Time for play

Photography by John Pettitt

We love playing.

We can go up the ladder
and down the slide.

We can play

hide-and-seek.

Can you see me?

I am hiding.

We can run races.

We run on the grass.

We can play

in the sandbox.

The cars can go

up and down the big hill.

Here are the blocks.

The little blocks

can go on the big blocks.

The tower goes up and up.

We can dress up.

Here we come.

We love playing.